ideals®
MOTHER'S DAY

There's nothing more precious
Than a mother's sweet prayer.
There's nothing more gracious
Than the love she will share.
There's nothing as strong
As the faith she declares;
And when things go wrong
We know that she cares.

Clay Harrison

ISBN 0-8249-1042-7

Publisher, Patricia A. Pingry
Editor, Ramona Richards
Art Director, David Lenz
Permissions, Kathleen Gilbert
Copy Editor, Susan DuBois

IDEALS—Vol. 43, No. 3 May MCMLXXXVI IDEALS (ISSN 0019-137X) is published eight times a year,
February, March, May, June, August, September, November, December
by IDEALS PUBLISHING, Nelson Place at Elm Hill Pike, Nashville, Tenn. 37214
Second class postage paid at Nashville, Tennessee, and additional mailing offices.
Copyright © MCMLXXXVI by IDEALS PUBLISHING.
POSTMASTER: Send address changes to Ideals, Post Office Box 148000, Nashville, Tenn. 37214
All rights reserved. Title IDEALS registered U.S. Patent Office.
Published simultaneously in Canada.

SINGLE ISSUE—$3.50
ONE-YEAR SUBSCRIPTION—eight consecutive issues as published—$15.95
TWO-YEAR SUBSCRIPTION—sixteen consecutive issues as published—$27.95
Outside U.S.A., add $4.00 per subscription year for postage and handling.

Front and back covers by Fred Sieb
Inside front cover by Fred Sieb
Inside back cover by Gerald Koser

Spring Bouquet

A vase of yellow daffodils
Placed in a living room,
Vies with the sun's amber waves
And dissipates all gloom.

A magic-like elixir
Fills every petalled cup,
Distills a pure sweet happiness
And builds the nectar up.

All outdoors comes inside,
Ignoring window sills;
Great beauty knows no boundary lines—
Nor golden daffodils.

Roy Z. Kemp

Photo Opposite
FIRST BOUQUET
H. Armstrong Roberts

My Mother's Flower Garden

My mother had a garden
With pinks and poppies tall
And purple morning glories
Climbing on a wall.

Snapdragons and larkspur
As blue as Heaven's skies,
Hollyhocks and mignonettes
That would have won a prize.

Pansies just like velvet,
Frail Canterbury bells,
Roses shared their secrets
With daisies who won't tell.

Folks would come to see it,
Ask how she made it grow,
Always she gave this reply,
"With love and spade and hoe."

Clara Cline Thompson

Flowering May

The apple blossoms, pink and white,
Perfume the month of May,
Across the meadows, emerald green,
And dance in bright array.

The dandelions yellow, gold,
Adorn the fields around,
They turn their faces toward the sun
Where rays of warmth are found.

The violets, so sweet and blue,
Peek out from 'neath the trees,
And smile with dainty tenderness
Amongst protective leaves.

The tulips and the garden flowers
Are blooming, bright and gay,
And everything is bursting forth
Now spring has come to stay.

Gertrude Rudberg

Country Chronicle

We always have lilacs in the house during spring. They rekindle memories of long-ago Mays when Mother made a ritual of keeping vases of fragrant lilacs on the marble-top stand in the parlor and on the antique walnut table in the sitting room. She brought in the May-time beauty and aroma of the clustered flowers. When the dew of evening fell on leaf and bloom, she would open the windows to let soft breezes sweep in more fragrance from bushes along an old stone wall. I like to think mothers are like the remembered lilacs of May's mild days. They endure.

Some of the lilacs at the home of my boyhood have survived more than a hundred years. Each generation had a role in making sure there would be lilacs near the door. The oldest hedge dates back to my grandfather who moved to the farm in 1848. The lilacs are still there. My father followed, and planted more lilacs. Then it was my turn to add to the growing lanes of bush and bloom.

When man had finished planting, nature stepped in. She scattered seeds in the pastures where no cows have grazed for a half century now. New bushes sprang up in meadows when

the family farm was transformed into a sanctuary for birds and wildlife—a haven for songbirds and frisking squirrels and a shelter for deer.

There are lilac lanes by the drive and by the stone walls separating gardens from barns and pastures. Lilacs grow along the creek that flows by the house, and along a hedge leading from the lawn to a gentle flowing stream which parallels the steel ribbons of the railroad tracks.

Lilacs are everywhere. There are white, purple, lavender and blue. They spread color and fragrance over the pastoral countryside.

Whitman wrote of the lilac with its "heart-shaped leaves." How fitting it is that I cherish the memories of Mother's bouquets of lilac blooms! They link fond, rich memories to the woman who nurtured me—the gingham-aproned woman who wiped away my tears when I stubbed a toe, and went on to guide me safely through my tender years.

Lansing Christman

My Rose of Memory

There's a creeping red rose vining over my door,
With petals like velvet in clusters of four.
It sends out a fragrance of lovely perfume
As all through the summer it hangs full of blooms.

Bright bees and butterflies swarm thick on its leaves
And the gay little hummingbirds flit through the breeze.
It is really a picture of nature in rhyme
And I watch my old creeper for hours at time.

I have many flowers of bright color and hue
That sparkle like gems when kissed by the dew.
But this cherished old creeper holds a place set apart,
For it weaves fondest memories deep down in my heart.

Hazel Elkins

Photo Opposite
"CRIMSON GLORY" ROSE
Richard Parker
Cyr Color

J. Harold Gwynne

Reverend J. Harold Gwynne, D.D., was born in Carmichaels, Pennsylvania, and educated at Princeton. He is an ordained minister of the Presbyterian Church and served pastorates in Pennsylvania and Ohio before retiring in 1966. Many of his writings are devoted to the spirit of Christian living, and his work has been featured in several anthologies, newspapers and magazines. He is the author of *The Rainbow Book of Bible Stories* and *Messages of Christian Faith*, which Ideals published in 1977.

Dr. Gwynne is a long-time contributor to *Ideals*, and we are proud to feature him as one of our Best-Loved Poets.

Crocuses in March

Bright clusters of golden crocus,
   And royal purple, too;
Neat borders of living color
   In March come peeping through!

When scarcely the snow has melted,
   And winter died away,
Then promptly these charming flowers
   Their dainty forms display.

Profusions of lovely flowers
   The summertime will bring;
But only you are, dear crocus,
   The harbinger of spring!

We fondly salute your spirit;
   Your coming always cheers!
For courage and hope are quickened
   When your fair form appears!

This Golden Summit
(For A Golden Wedding Anniversary)

This golden summit where you stand
    Commands a vista far and wide,
A glorious view of yon far land
    You've traveled over side by side.

In life's fair spring your hearts were wed,
    And love's sweet dreams were bright and true.
You faced the road that stretched ahead,
    And walked the path God chose for you.

Rich joys and blessings you have known.
    You've sought for beauty, truth, and right.
Both wise and gentle you have grown.
    In God's good time you've scaled the height.

Your host of friends now honor you.
    Your children rise and call you blest.
They wish you joy in all you do,
    And hope for you the very best.

You've won at last by God's good grace
    This golden summit, fair and grand,
Whence you behold His smiling face,
    And glimpse beyond His promised land!

Three Precious Words

Three precious words to us are given;
These gems are Mother, Home, and Heaven.

Be wise and take them to your heart,
And never more let them depart.

For Mother is the name for Love,
Sent from the Father God above.

And Home the place that Mother makes,
In love and joy for our dear sakes;

While Heaven itself is our true Home,
From whence God's children never roam.

Three precious words—O may they shine
Forever in your heart and mine!

Garden Song

Whoever tends a garden
Has many gentle friends:

The beauty of the morning,
The peace when daytime ends,

The birds their carols singing,
The flowers of lovely hue,

The tender plants upspringing,
The leafy foliage new,

The dew, the rain, the sunshine,
The soft and verdant sod,

The deep and mystic feeling
Of walking close with God!

Bleeding Hearts

Each time I see thee, Bleeding Hearts,
A wave of tender feeling starts,

That takes me back across the years
To boyhood days of smiles and tears.

I see a garden, quaint and fair,
With Grandma tending flowers there.

She dearly loved thee, dainty flower—
The fairest in her garden bower.

Your heart-shaped pendants, row on row,
The purest pink and white did show.

They seemed so real, so pure, so sweet;
Their life-blood flowed with every beat!

Dear Bleeding Hearts, I've loved you so,
Through all the years from long ago.

For in your pretty forms I see
Those days long past, that seem to be.

Photo Overleaf
MENDOCINO COAST
Ed Cooper

Wild Flowers

Today the wild, small flowers
Are everywhere I look,
They dot the fields and foothills
And edge a singing brook.
They saunter down a hillside
And pause beside a tree,
Bright spots of instant beauty
So happy and carefree.

Like any bird that soars above
Across the heavens blue,
Enjoying warmth and little winds
And early morning dew.
The purple of wild asters,
The Indian paintbrush flames,
The gold of dancing daisies
The Queen Anne's lace remains.

They charm away quiet hours
Where few will ever pass,
But their splendor some will behold
Who catch a glimpse at last,
Of flowers bright as sunshine
And as joyous as a song,
That grace the hills and fields
For acres, on and on!

Vera Laurel Hoffman

Like Mother Used to Make

The other day I read in a readers'-request column this plea: "Can someone please tell me how to make old-fashioned apple strudel? I have the recipe my mother used, but somehow my apple strudel never turns out the way hers did, and I'm wondering what I could be doing wrong."

Will she ever find the secret? I, too, wondered. No matter how many readers try to help her, how many suggestions she receives about the extra dash of sugar, the freshness of the butter, the temperature of the oven, the timing of the baking, will anyone ever be able to reproduce the magic formula that was her mother's and hers alone?

Like Mother used to make...Bakers long have claimed the slogan; advertisers have lured us with it to their pickles and catsups and jellies and jams.

Like Mother used to make...The very words conjure up a kitchen where a woman toils lovingly to fashion her family's favorite dishes. It paints a nostalgic picture of children flocking around wanting to help—to beat the eggs, to stir the batter, to roll out the pie-crust, to cut the cookies, to handle the bread dough. It re-creates a hundred small, significant scenes—of people who come sniffing into a kitchen, begging a taste of this, a nibble of that, peering into the oven and pleading, "Something smells good. Is supper ready? I'm starved."

Like Mother used to make...The cheese soufflé. The nut bread. The chicken casserole. The potato pancakes. The cherry pie. The Christmas plum pudding.

Recipes we have aplenty, passed along to daughters, presented to sons' brides. "Johnny is awfully fond of upside-down cake. I always made it this way." And eagerly the young wife follows directions, does her best to duplicate that special dish. But she knows, even when he's too polite to tell her, that something is different about it. Whatever her skills or practice, something is missing, some rare, lost ingredient that not even the best-intentioned cook can supply.

Because a mother stirs a little bit of herself into everything she cooks for her family. Unseen, all unsuspected, into the bowl goes the

subtle flavor of her personality—the way she thinks and feels, the way she laughs or tilts her head or scolds. And into this dish of hers, too, go the whole measure and taste of the home—the way the dining room used to look when the lamps were lighted, the sound of family voices, the laughter, the quarrels, the memories.

These are the ingredients we lack when we try to reproduce the dish that Mother used to make. These are her secret spices. They are not for sale, and they can't be passed along.

Yet every woman who enters a kitchen carries with her a rare and precious store of her own. The flavor of *herself* in relation to her children, the warmth and tang and savor of her own household. Daily, inescapably, without ever realizing it, all of us are blending these inimitable components into other dishes, into other lives.

So that one day our children, too, will say, "My mother used to make the most wonderful peach cobbler. I can't make it come out the same, no matter how hard I try!"

Marjorie Holmes

Photo Overleaf
"LIKE MOTHER USED TO MAKE"
Fred Sieb

Grandmother's Quilt

On this Monday morning—
  with the heady scent of lilacs
    filling the air,

I begin my spring cleaning.

The hall closet is first—
  where piles of ill-folded blankets
    mountains of lumpy pillows
plummet onto the floor
  each time the door is opened.

I pull snatches
  of satin trim,
make piles of like colors
  for trips to the washer.

Then from a back corner,
  it tumbles down on me—

my grandmother's quilt.

I finger the fine stitches,
  remembering Grandma's gnarled knuckles
    big-eyed needles.

I recognize the pieces:
  lavender of an Easter dress long-forgotten
  red print from my sister's favorite blouse
  a patch of blue flowers formerly a pocket
    on Mother's apron.

I bury my face in the quilt.

It smells faintly of
  dust
    soap
      cedar.

And I remember countless cold nights
  when Grandma layered me
    in colorful warmth.

I carry the quilt
  to the line,
squinting into springtime sun
  as I clothespin yellowing corners.

And while I watch breezes blow
  these bits of colored cloth,
I realize how much my life
  is like this quilt—

patterned with
  dark patches
  bright splashes

stitched together with
  God's patience
    persistence
      love.

Mary Lou Carney

The Patchwork Quilt

I have a lovely patchwork quilt
That Mother made for me.
It brightens up my life because
It's rich in memory.

Whenever days are dark and long
I trace each lovely piece
That Mom so lovingly did sew
And my heart finds release.

For everywhere along the quilt
Familiar pieces lie,
Reminding me of youthful dreams
In happy days gone by.

Each pretty pattern brings to mind
Some suit or dress I wore
To parties or to Sunday school
In those dear days of yore.

For Mother saved each tiny scrap
And pieced them patiently,
To make this lovely patchwork quilt
So lovingly for me.

Carice Williams

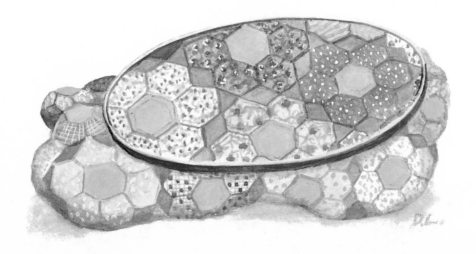

A Loaf of Mother's Bread

I have heard them speak of biscuits,
   "Like my mother used to make."
I have heard them tell of cookies,
   Apple pie and angel cake;
But for good old joy in eating
   When the hungry must be fed,
I'll just take some homemade butter
   And a loaf of Mother's bread.

There was love went in the mixing
   And the kneading of the dough.
There was care went in the watching,
   That the fire burned just so.
There was hearty satisfaction,
   When she took them, golden-brown,
From the oven to the table
   And there turned them upside-down.

Then she greased them well with butter,
   Bottom, sides and top and ends;
And to see them there a-cooling,
   Was like greeting old-time friends.
And I'd give a baker's dozen
   Of the loaves which now I spread,
For a bit of homemade butter
   And a loaf of "Mother's bread."

W. Earlington Whitney

Something in the Heart

Whenever I smell fresh blueberry pie
Still warm from the oven's deep rack,
I am lost on a wave of nostalgic joy
That carries me swiftly back

To a kitchen I haven't seen in years.
Where the table was always spread,
And the air was fragrant every day
With mother's homemade bread.

I smile remembering the noisy lad
Who breathlessly took his place
At every meal in the nick of time
Before the start of grace.

The years are many that run between
And the lad that I used to know
Has long since grown to manhood
By every outward show;

Yet deep within where mem'ry dwells
I keep a place apart
Where age can never matter much
To one still young at heart.

Viney Wilder Endicott

Canning Time

Tomatoes yellow, red and green
  In baskets on the floor;
Squash and peppers in the sink
  And cucumbers galore.

Jars all washed and shiny-bright;
  Spices near at hand;
Corn, cut fresh from off the cob,
  Waiting to be canned.

Slender carrots, bright orange-gold,
  Onions juicy-sweet,
Green beans, wax beans, melon rind
  And all things good to eat.

Apples blushing scarlet red,
  Apricots so mellow,
Peaches sweet and rosy-pink,
  Quinces ripe and yellow.

Kraut processing in a crock,
  Pickles in the brine;
Spicy fragrance in the house—
  It's Mother's canning time!

Mrs. Paul E. King

Complaint

My mom has been housecleaning now
For almost two whole weeks,
And in our attic things are piled
In awful stacks and peaks.

My dad says he could open shop
With all that's in that place,
And give the merchants in our town
A really lively chase!

Gee, Dad was mad the day he found
His nice soft easy chair
Had been removed in favor of
A needlepoint affair.

But he was even more put out
To see the sofa go,
And have a love seat move right in,
And boy, he told Mom so!

But Dad is not the only one
Who feels he's been abused.
I have a few complaints myself
The way my room's been used.

The drawers and closets have been cleaned
Till nothing's left at all!
My favorite baseball players have
Been banished from the wall.

My bag of marbles, too, is gone,
And so's my roll of string;
They've disappeared just like the tooth
I saved from way last spring!

Our house is turned clean inside out,
Mom's busy as a bee.
I'm sure she never stops to think
It's tough on Dad and me!

Viney Wilder Endicott

The Songs My Mother Sang

I often catch vague fragments of a tune,
Or haunting airs, like notes the gray doves croon,
Which bring back boyhood's happy time of June,
    And songs my mother sang.

The melodies she loved the best to sing,
Beneath the elms, at work down at the spring,
Now faintly float to me on fancy's wing,
    The songs my mother sang.

I hear from the old orchard, as the breeze
Wafts fragrance from the snow-white locust trees,
And pink-tipped apple blossoms lure the bees,
    The songs my mother sang.

As pictures of the past before me throng
I see her there, when winter nights are long,
Before the wood fire, rocking; then a song
    Again I hear her sing.

Sometimes her guest was sorrow, sometimes pain:
She looked to Him who will the weak sustain;
Her soul triumphant rose in sweet refrain
    In songs she loved to sing.

The grass for years upon her grave has grown;
Familiar paths she trod I walk alone,
But very near she seems when comes a tone
    From songs she used to sing.

Clyde Edwin Tuck

The Reading Mother

I had a mother who read to me
Sagas of pirates who scoured the sea,
Cutlasses clenched in their yellow teeth,
"Blackbirds" stowed in the hold beneath.

I had a mother who read me lays
Of ancient and gallant and golden days;
Stories of Marmion and Ivanhoe,
Which every child has a right to know.

I had a mother who read me tales
Of Gelert, the hound of the hills of Wales,
True to his trust till his tragic death,
Faithfulness blended with his final breath.

I had a mother who read me the things
That wholesome life to a child's heart brings,
Stories that stir with an upward touch,
Oh, that each mother of children were such!

You may have tangible wealth untold;
Caskets of jewels and coffers of gold.
Richer than I you can never be—
I had a mother who read to me.

Strickland Gillilan

Grandma's Parlor

My grandma had a parlor
That always seemed to stay
In neat and perfect order
'Cause no one there could play.

It seemed sort of gloomy
With chairs of black horsehair,
And yet, each dainty doily
Shone white most everywhere.

The pictures on the mantlepiece
Were framed in fancy gold.
A clock, an ancient timepiece,
Struck notes that sounded old.

The wood stove in the center
Was seldom used at all,
Except in coldest weather
And spring and early fall.

And on the pinewood table
An oil lamp burnt so bright,
As she would read the Bible
To teach us what was right.

The organ in the corner
Was seldom ever played
Unless the country preacher
Would ask her, after he prayed.

Yes, Grandma had a parlor,
That I remember well,
And 'cause it's filled with folklore,
I think that I should tell.

Gertrude Rudberg

Rainy Day Remembrance

Long ago, when a rainy day
Would interrupt my outdoor play,
Mom would let me sort quilt blocks
And happily dig in her button-box.

I'd play dress-up in cast-off shoes
And from catalogs she'd help me choose
Paper dolls to cut just so,
Then we'd make some cookie dough.

The rainy days turned out just fine;
I'm glad I was young in a simpler time,
And bless my mother of old-fashioned ways,
And her infinite patience on rainy days.

Elsie Mae Watkins

Three Little Ladies

Three little ladies
Went strolling one day,
Dressed "just like Mommy"
When she goes away.

With oodles of jewelry
And heels, oh so high
They wobbled and giggled
'Til they caught every eye.

Then nodding politely
"Good morning," said they.
"We thought we'd go strolling;
It's a beautiful day."

So dressed in high fashion
They went on their way,
Three little ladies
Playing "Mommy" today.

Claribel Ream

Mother's Day Luncheon
Tropical Chicken Salad
Makes 4 servings

4 cups cooked chicken, cut in ½-inch cubes
1 cup diced celery
1 cup green seedless grapes, halved
¾ cup toasted, slivered almonds
½ cup mayonnaise
2 tablespoons milk
1 tablespoon sugar
1 tablespoon chopped fresh parsley
  Salt and white pepper
1 pineapple
  Almond slivers
  Leaf lettuce
  Assorted fresh fruit

Combine the first 8 ingredients in a mixing bowl. Season to taste with salt and pepper; chill well. Cut the pineapple in quarters, lengthwise, keeping the leaves intact. Remove core and dice pineapple pulp; set aside. Fill each shell with chicken salad; sprinkle with almonds. Place each shell on a plate lined with lettuce; surround with diced pineapple and assorted fresh fruit. Serve chilled.

Spiced Iced Tea

5 cups water
2 strips lemon rind
6 whole cloves
1 1½-inch cinnamon stick
3 allspice berries
3 tablespoons tea leaves
4 cinnamon sticks
4 orange peel spirals, studded with
  whole cloves

Combine water, lemon rind, cloves, cinnamon stick, and allspice in a saucepan; bring to a boil. Simmer for 10 minutes. Pour hot mixture over tea leaves; set aside for 5 minutes. Strain into a pitcher; refrigerate until cold. Pour tea into 4 glasses filled with crushed ice. Garnish with cinnamon sticks and orange rind spirals.

Strawberry Muffins

¼ cup butter
½ cup sugar
1 egg
1½ cups flour
½ teaspoon salt
2 teaspoons baking powder
½ cup milk
1 cup sliced fresh strawberries (or fruit of your choice)

Preheat oven to 350⁰. Cream together the butter and sugar in a mixing bowl until light and fluffy. Add egg; mix lightly. Sift flour, salt, and baking powder together; add alternately with milk to butter mixture. Stir just to blend; fold in the berries. Spoon batter into 12 greased muffin tins. Sprinkle each with granulated sugar. Bake for 15 to 20 minutes or until a cake tester inserted in center comes out clean.

Mother and Her Secret

Al Capp

You hear a lot about kids fooling their mothers, but you hardly ever hear of a mother fooling her kids. But I knew one who did. Mine. But in the end we found out the truth about her.

We grew up during the Depression. Now kids today may not know what a depression means. It doesn't mean one car in the family and steak once a week, even if that is as ghastly a life as kids today can imagine. The Depression meant no shoes, no meat and barely enough shelter—with a fighting chance that the whole family would be evicted onto the sidewalk. That was the Depression. And it was harder still because our father had left us.

Well, all through those grim years my mother managed to keep her four children fed, sheltered, clothed, and in school. Her hair turned white before she was 35. She was cheerful enough, but her eyes had a sort of haunted look. She never had any pretty clothes or good times.

When we four grew up, we all did well enough to pool a fairly handsome hunk of cash to send Mom each week, so that what-

ever years she had left from about 50 on would be different from the years before. But we were all kind of disappointed in Mom's new life. She didn't move into a new home; she said she was perfectly comfortable in the old one. She didn't hire any help to take her off her feet; she said she liked doing housework. She didn't buy any pretty clothes. She kept delaying the vacations to Florida or to Europe that we planned for her—until we gave up planning. Still, that weekly check came in, and, as we four figured it, since she didn't spend more than a fraction of it each week she must have saved a considerable amount by the time she died some 20 years later.

Well, when we went through her papers we found that Mom was broke! Those checks had been spent the instant they arrived. On what? As soon as we kids were off her back, Mom had secretly arranged with a refugee outfit to ship her four war orphans from Europe. She'd set them up in a home near hers, and for 20 years she'd educated them, seen them through sickness and teen-age problems, and, in two cases, into marriage.

She never told us about the four new kids. I guess she wasn't sure we'd approve of her going through the whole mess all over again. I'm not sure we would have, either. You see, it isn't easy for kids who've grown up seeing their mothers knock themselves out half their lives to raise them to understand that motherhood is a sort of incurable condition.

Mother's Prayer

Dear God,
This prayer is very old.
You hear it every day
From lips of mothers everywhere
In all the tongues that pray.

Behold these children round my knee
Whose steps do falter still,
Unhurt by fears or sorrows yet,
Untouched by hatred's chill.

How well you know what's in my mind,
And what I'm going to ask.
It's just that You will guide my hand
In my momentous task.

I feel so very awed within
At what I have to do
To help them be the kind of folk
Who, too, will turn to You.

Margaret Rorke

When God Created Sun and Stars

Katherine Edelman

Of all the love that has been known
Since time and earth began,
Of all the faith that has been shown
Since God created man,
Of all the noble, stirring deeds
That grace the written page,
A mother's boundless love and faith
Stand out through every age.

Her deeds have moved the
    sternest hearts
To wonder and to tears,
Her love has kindled faith and trust
Through all the changing years;
Her sacrifice, unselfishness,
Her trust through praise or blame
Have shrined her in the hearts of all
And glorified her name.

For though the world may
    frown or sneer,
Though failure may be ours,
Her love still folds, encircles us,
A rosary of flowers;
A comforting, sustaining force,
A star that brightly gleams,
That softens every care and hurt,
And shares our hopes and dreams.

The Adventures of Peter Rabbit

Once upon a time there were four little Rabbits, and their names were — Flopsy, Mopsy, Cotton-tail, and Peter. They lived with their Mother in a sand-bank, underneath the root of a very big fir tree.

"Now, my dears," said old Mrs. Rabbit one morning, "you may go into the fields or down the lane, but don't go into Mr. McGregor's garden: your Father had an accident there; he was put in a pie by Mrs. McGregor.

"Now run along, and don't get into mischief. I am going out."

Then old Mrs. Rabbit took a basket and her umbrella, and went through the woods to the baker's. She bought a loaf of brown bread and five currant buns.

Flopsy, Mopsy, and Cotton-tail, who were good little bunnies, went down the lane to gather blackberries; but Peter, who was very naughty, ran straight away to Mr. McGregor's garden, and squeezed under the gate!

First he ate some lettuces and some French beans; and then he ate some radishes; and then, feeling rather sick, he went to look for some parsley.

But round the end of a cucumber frame, whom should he meet but Mr. McGregor! Mr. McGregor was on his hands and knees planting out young cabbages, but he jumped up and ran after Peter, waving a rake and calling out, "Stop thief!"

Peter was most dreadfully frightened; he rushed all over the garden, for he had forgotten the way back to the gate. He lost one of his shoes among the cabbages, and the other shoe amongst the potatoes. After losing them, he ran on four legs and went faster, so that I think he might have gotten away altogether if he had not unfortunately run into a gooseberry net, and got caught by the large buttons on his jacket. It was a blue jacket with brass buttons, quite new.

Peter gave himself up for lost, and shed big tears; but his sobs were overheard by some friendly sparrows, who flew to him in great excitement, and implored him to exert himself.

Mr. McGregor came up with a sieve, which he intended to pop upon the top of Peter; but Peter wriggled out just in time, leaving his jacket behind him.

Mr. McGregor hung up the little jacket and the shoes for a scare-crow to frighten the blackbirds.

Peter never stopped running or looked behind him till he got home to the big fir tree.

He was so tired that he flopped down upon the nice soft sand on the floor of

the rabbit-hole and shut his eyes. His mother was busy cooking; she wondered what he had done with his clothes. It was the second little jacket and pair of shoes that Peter had lost in a fortnight!

I am sorry to say that Peter was not very well during the evening.

His mother put him to bed, and made some camomile tea; and she gave a dose of it to Peter!

"One table-spoonful to be taken at bed-time."

But Flopsy, Mopsy, and Cotton-tail had bread and milk and blackberries for supper.

Beatrix Potter

Old Treasures

Daughter sees but a faded rose—

But for mother a sunny garden grows,
And a radiant girl in gown of white
Waits for her lover with face alight.

A tiny shoe with a button missed—

But mother sees the feet she kissed,
Rosy and sweet and satin-soft
That she bathed, cuddled and dressed so oft.

A lock of hair with a glint of sun—

But for mother again the day is done,
And she cradles the sleepy golden head
As she sings to the baby ready for bed.

A rose, a shoe, a lock of hair,
That's all that daughter sees lying there,

But to mother the memories live and glow
Out of the dust of long ago.

And by and by the maiden fair
Will count her treasures hid somewhere,
For our precious things with the years must go,
But memory keeps them. I'm glad it's so.

Mildred M. North

Tomorrow
I'll Clean The Attic

"Tomorrow I'll clean the attic," I said,
And meant it with all my heart.
"I'll get up early with suds and broom,
And make a wonderful start.

"I'll throw away all of those useless things
We've kept for ever so long."
So I tackled the job the very next day,
Humming a brave little song.

But I hadn't thought of the rocking horse,
Or the treasured, childish games,
Or the little ship carved by a faraway lad,
Today the designer of planes.

And I hadn't thought of the catcher's mitt,
Or the Eskimo doll that could cry!
Oh, I had forgotten what attics can do
To a person as weak as I!

"Tomorrow I'll clean the attic," I said,
"And everything has to go!"
Tomorrow? I'll mean it with all my heart
In a hundred years or so.

Alice Hansche Mortenson

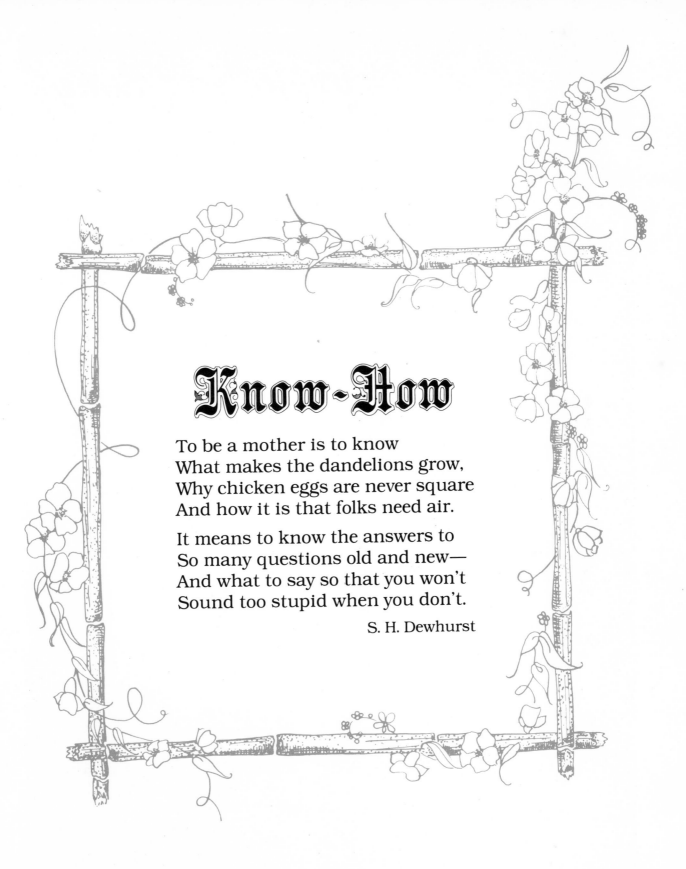

Know-How

To be a mother is to know
What makes the dandelions grow,
Why chicken eggs are never square
And how it is that folks need air.

It means to know the answers to
So many questions old and new—
And what to say so that you won't
Sound too stupid when you don't.

S. H. Dewhurst

New Mother's Song

My darling, don't cry,
Because you've been born.
You'll see hummingbirds fly
In this world that you scorn
So vociferously now.

You'll touch tiny oak leaves
As soft on the bough
As your palm that receives
These kisses of mine.

You'll see mountains and rain
And smell cedar and pine—
Oh, my small, don't complain,
For I tell you most true,
And my honor I'm giving,
Any world that holds you
Is a good world for living.

Jane Merchant

A Mother's Memory

That squeezed and stemless first bouquet
Outshines the florist's prize today.
The pangs of mem'ry fairly shout
Of teeth that came and then came out,
Of school days, scouts, and baseball games,
Recitals, plays—and many names,
Beclouded recollection skims
For adding little hers and hims—
Companions of the yesteryear
To those whose childhood I hold dear.

The holidays while they grew,
The birthday celebrations too,
Their strengths, their quirks, their little flaws,
Their fears and hurts that gave me pause.
And then those graduation days
When they attained their grown-up phase!
But never will their lives outride
Their mother's worry or her pride.
Young mothers, heed the bad . . . the bliss;
Your time will come to reminisce.

Margaret Rorke

Photo Overleaf
FRIENDSHIP GARDEN
Fred Dole

GROWING SEASONS

Motherhood. Plain and simple eloquence, wrapped up in a word. It's not so much being as becoming. A passage through the seasons of the heart. A journey universal yet unique.

She is the first to know of his existence in the flickering flutter so like a butterfly's wing. She nourishes and tends from the beginning and, when the time is right, brings forth the full-grown infant; potential only she can see at first. Then the task begins. The cultivating season is a trying time. Night and daytime blend into one. Hours once spent elsewhere are passed in pacing, rocking, lullabying, wishing suns to rise. The rewards are small—a smile, a grinning gurgle, fingers wound tightly in her hair. Somehow that's enough—for now.

Months are strung together like the beads upon a chain, and soon the necklace spans a year. She watches as the fledgling turns away and wobbles from her arms. Small, deliberate steps at first, but she knows it is beginning. The seasons change. The separation cannot be denied. This is what it's all about. She knows, but still it's hard.

The chubby arms and chunky legs soon take control. Running, skipping, jumping, hopping. Never still, never silent, never satisfied with what is near. She must hold him in her heart these days, this bubbling brook of energy. Her arms are too confining.

When did the puppy become a colt? Long legs leaping in the sun. "Oh, Mama look! Oh, Mama see! Oh, Mama watch me, watch me!" How many years since the days of butterfly wings fluttering inside? He's still becoming what he is to be, little by little. She is changing, too, growing through the seasons of her son.

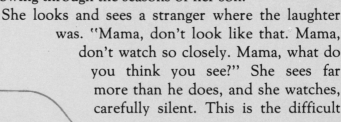

She looks and sees a stranger where the laughter was. "Mama, don't look like that. Mama, don't watch so closely. Mama, what do you think you see?" She sees far more than he does, and she watches, carefully silent. This is the difficult

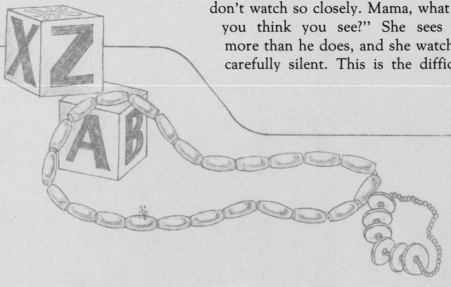

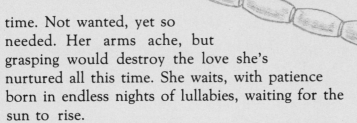

time. Not wanted, yet so needed. Her arms ache, but grasping would destroy the love she's nurtured all this time. She waits, with patience born in endless nights of lullabies, waiting for the sun to rise.

The yearning years pass and in their place a tentative time arrives. "Mama, are you still my friend? Mama, will you always be there? Mama, you look different." And in her heart she knows it was not she who changed. He seeks her out to share a broken heart, and because she knows the feeling, she can help. "Oh, Mama, you're so wise." She strains to hide a smile and sends him on his way to face his fear.

One day, when she's not looking, independence snatches him away. "Wish me well, Mama." But it hurts to watch him go. Is this what all that leaving was about? Somehow, the training doesn't seem enough. Will she ever master this tough role?

The seasons turn again. What has she become? Who needs her? What good was all the caring and dreaming when the dream is gone? A letter now and then, a phone call here and there. The empty arms, the empty nest cry out! What is she now?

"Oh Mama, look! Oh Mama, see! Oh Mama, watch him, just like me!" The lost returned in miniature. Brought back to empty arms. Old feelings flutter back to life; laughter brought by dimpled cheeks. "Gramma, Gramma! Lookit, lookit me!"

Now it's come full circle. Seasons turning around her son. The wondering and the dreams are filled with hope again. She knows what she's been through these years was worth it all—laughter, tears, sorrow, joy. Anxiety has turned to peace; emptiness to fulfillment. Motherhood has earned its own rewards—another growing season of the heart.

Pamela Kennedy

Mother's Day Gift

I went into a shop, Mom,
Today, all by myself,
And as I looked around, Mom,
I saw upon a shelf
A pretty hat of straw, Mom,
The kind you always liked.
And as I looked it over,
It even was your size.

It had a lacy tie, Mom,
And large red flowers, too;
It was a pretty hat, Mom,
The kind that you would choose.
So, since it's Mother's Day, Mom,
And I love you so much,
I bought this hat for you, Mom,
As a token of my love.

Loise Pinkerton Fritz

The Little Hand
That I Once Held

Once she was just a tiny tot,
Knee-high as he is now.
'Twas years ago, and yet it seems
Like yesterday, somehow.
She'd place her little hand in mine
And through the fields we'd walk.
Just God and I fully understood
The many joys she brought.

We trampled through the forest green
And down along the creek,
And when we'd find a bunny's nest,
She'd take a little peek.
We wandered where the wild flowers grew,
She'd pick a sweet bouquet.
"I'll give them to my mommy
'Cause I love her best," she'd say.

Today, alone, I stood and watched
Them walking hand-in-hand—
The little girl, now quite grown up,
And a small freckled-faced lad.
Barefooted through the fields they roamed;
He looked at her and smiled;
Yes, the little hand that I once held
Now led another child.

Loise Pinkerton Fritz

Woodland Path

I walked along a woodland path,
Sweet silence all around.
Wild flowers bloomed profusely there;
Wild strawberries decked the ground.

Bright fireweed bloomed, and asters, too;
And the clover smelled so sweet,
And with pink Indian paintbrushes
The decor was complete.

A chipmunk scampered gaily by,
A wild bird trilled a note.
And overhead, through sunlit leaves,
I saw the white clouds float.

I picked some strawberries, ripe and red,
A feast fit for a king.
And kneeling there, it seemed I heard
All of Nature sing!

Elma Helgason

Readers' Reflections

A Little Boy's Kisses

A little boy's kiss is a transient thing—
A rose in full bloom; a moth on the wing.

One kiss is spontaneous, flavored with milk.
Another is sleep-covered, texture of silk.

A kiss born of duty, delivered in haste—
His life's so exciting, there's no time to waste.

Assorted endearments; to bribe or atone;
His thanks for some toy he's been begging to own.

I treasure them all, for I'm certain of this—
Too soon he will feel that it's "sissy" to kiss!

Norma J. Lagoe
Minoa, New York

Editor's Note: Readers are invited to submit poetry, short anecdotes, and humorous reflections on life for possible publication in future *Ideals* issues. Please send copies only; manuscripts will not be returned. Writers will receive $10 for each published submission. Send materials to "Readers' Reflections," Ideals Publishing, Nelson Place at Elm Hill Pike, Nashville, Tennessee 37214.

A Home

It's just a small house,
    humble and bare,
But I see warm lights and hear
    laughter in there.
There are flowers, a garden and
    wood in a stack
There is plenty of grass,
    and a barn in the back.

It's just a small house, but it's
    clean and it's neat.
It's filled with much love
    and children so sweet.
There's a tree-house to climb
    and kittens to pet
A sand box and tire-swing,
    not fancy and yet
The wealth can't be measured
    in silver or gold
There are kisses and hugs and
    strong arms that hold.

It's just a small house,
    humble and bare
But you know it's a home
    with all the love there!

Marilyn J. Ferguson
West Salem, Ohio

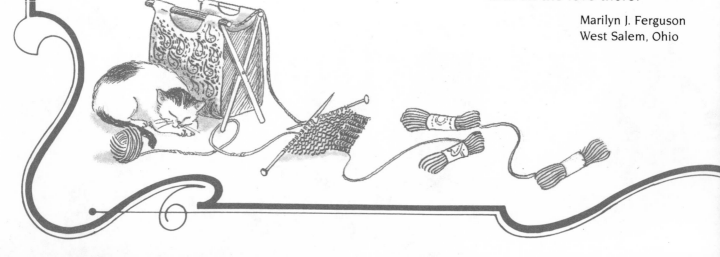

A Mother Gives Thanks

Thank You, Lord, for clothes to wash
Or dirty dishes in the sink,
For little voices in the night
Calling for another drink.

Thank You, too, for stains and dirt
Smeared on towels that once were clean;
For that stack of mending, Lord,
Piled high upon my sewing machine.

Thank You for those sticky spills
Upon the floor that I just scrubbed,
For toothpaste tubes without lids
And dirty rings around the tub.

Forgive me, Lord, if I should complain
Of these; instead use them to remind
Of the one You've placed within my care—
Thank You, Lord, for this child of mine!

Ann S. Dougherty
Charleston, South Carolina

A Mother's Day Wish

Although I wish I could join you there,
Bright flowers let you know I care.
My bouquet I send to you to say,
"Have a Happy Mother's Day."
Don't feel that you are all alone.
My thoughts are there within your home.
So on your very special day,
Think not of me as miles away,
For in my heart I am there with you,
And you can be here with me, too.

Al Hearin
Jacksonville, Florida

Her Magic

As a little boy,
Running through the fields,
Never being careful,
Never knowing when to yield,

I'd chase a buzzing bee,
Not thinking of any harm,
Then just before I knew it,
He went and stung my arm!

I went crying to the house,
Knowing she'd be there,
I guess that Mom's the answer,
To every child's prayer.

She looked upon my wound,
And pulled the stinger out,
It made me feel much better,
I didn't even have to pout.

She kissed away the hurt,
No longer seeming tragic,
Not even medicine the doctor has,
Compares to Mother's magic!

Bruce Benzel
Fond du Lac, Wisconsin

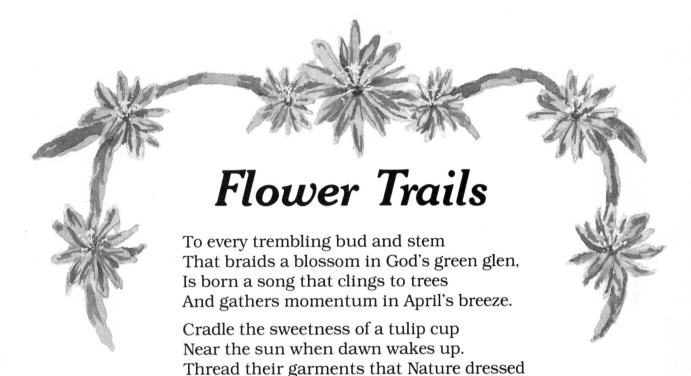

Flower Trails

To every trembling bud and stem
That braids a blossom in God's green glen,
Is born a song that clings to trees
And gathers momentum in April's breeze.

Cradle the sweetness of a tulip cup
Near the sun when dawn wakes up.
Thread their garments that Nature dressed
With deeds of fire and creativeness.

Forge with beauty an elegant vine
That foliage tossed with blooms of wine.
Weave in a meadow where lilacs feed
A touch of scarlet and camellia seed.

Trumpet in fields that are spendor tossed
With stems of gold and horns of frost.
Welcome the flowers that are temple blessed
For they dwell in gardens that God caressed.

Wayne B. Dayton

My Little Garden

I have a little garden.
It is freshly plowed each spring,
And then is duly planted
With a bit of everything.

I tend to my little garden
Before the morning sun gets hot,
Then stop to pull up an onion
To flavor the stew in the pot.

I believe that my little garden
Is therapy for my soul,
It's an Eden, a hobby, a challenge,
A salubrious salad bowl.

From out of my little garden
Come potatoes, peppers, and peas
To grace the dinner table, and remind me
Of God's gifts that never cease.

Maye Georgeson

Inside My Garden Gate

I'm grateful for a garden
Where I can walk about,
To mingle with the growing things
From tender leaf to sprout.

Where I can breathe the fragrance
Of roses sweet and fair,
And nourish pink geraniums
And lilies growing there.

I feel secure and happy
It's much like coming home.
There's a sacred kind of passion
All about me while I roam

Through the pathways of my garden,
Where fantastic wonders wait.
I'm enraptured by these miracles
Inside my garden gate.

Verna Sparks

Wildflowers

From hollow, hill, and rugged slope
They rise from leafy beds,
And bloom in rainbow-colored hues
Some nod their dappled heads.

Mayapples lift their emerald hats
Like gallant little skippers,
An orchid waltzing with the breeze
Shakes dewdrops from her slippers.

Honeysuckles are dressing up
In flaming tangerine,
Minty catnip scents the air
Along the rushing stream.

Honeybees are buzzing around
A lofty sourwood tree,
Crimson berries nestle amidst
The leaves of mountain tea.

Majestic pines are whispering
'Cause wrens are nesting there,
The dogwood trees are snowy white
And God is everywhere!

Loy C. Guy

Photo Opposite
PT. REYES SEASHORE
Ed Cooper

The Merry Month of May

May is a month for memories. It evokes thoughts of soft breezes, balmy weather, fragrant flowers, colorful May baskets and Mother's Day. May Day celebrations started with the Celts, who marked the birthday of their god, Belenos, with a festival called *Beltane*. Because he was associated with fire and the sun, they extinguished all their house fires, started a gigantic bonfire on a hilltop, and re-lit all their fires from it. They selected a tree, usually a hawthorne or May tree and set it up in the center of the village. They decorated it with flowers and used it as the focal point for special dances and celebrations. Many of their ceremonies were done to encourage the growth of their crops in the warmth of the summer sun.

The Romans also celebrated this time of the year. They held spring festivals to honor *Flora*, their goddess of flowers, and May Day was considered so special that they even gave their slaves the day off. Collecting flowers, feasting and dancing around a centrally placed tree were all part of their festivities, too.

During the Middle Ages, May Day continued to be a time of celebration in England and was even declared a public holiday. People went *a-maying* into the woods, gathering flowers and boughs to carry in processions. Young women rubbed morning dew on their faces to promote healthy complexions.

The May tree now became the *maypole* and was set up in a prominent place in the town. People decorated it with single flowers, garlands and streamers. Some maypoles were even left standing year-round. To add to the gaiety, people wore wreaths in their hair, sewed ribbons and bells on their clothes and exchanged baskets of flowers. Around the maypole, there were games and contests, music and dances. A favorite, the morris dance, included stamping steps said to awaken the sleeping spirits of the soil.

Both men and women enjoyed marching in the May Day processions. In the eighteenth century, even chimney sweeps marched, wearing their sooty clothes. They followed a man called *Jack-in-the-Green*, who was decorated with green tree branches and flowers and who represented spring. The chimney sweeps symbolized the dark winter days which had passed.

There was always a Queen of the May. She was an example of the best of some quality—the prettiest, the youngest, the most respected. She and her attendants sat in a place of honor and the queen awarded prizes to the winners of the games.

Special dishes and drinks were prepared, usually with a green theme. There were parsley breads, green vegetables, green cider and even a green gingerbread man representing Jack-in-the-Green. All this reinforced that people were celebrating the re-awakening of the earth.

Today, May is mainly associated with Mother's Day. Setting aside a special day to honor mothers has some history, too. The English celebrated a *Mothering Sunday* as far back as the seventeenth century. At this time young people who worked a distance from their home were given off the fourth Sunday in Lent so they could visit their parents and take them presents. This custom evolved from the tradition of returning to a parish *mother* church the one day in Lent when feasting and fun were allowed.

In the United States, President Woodrow Wilson proclaimed an official day of recognition for mothers in 1914. This is a day to outwardly demonstrate appreciation for the women who give so much of themselves to their children. Some people buy gifts; others, spurning commercialism, give their time and themselves.

There is a special quality to the month of May. Maypoles and May baskets are no longer common, but people still celebrate the arrival of spring. The bursting of bud to flower and the anticipation of summer's warmth and bounty provide a sense of hope after a long, cold winter.

Anne Eccles

Maytime

Have you ever gone out walking
In the early month of May?
When the skies are blue all over,
And the birds have come to stay?

When the flower buds are bursting
And their fragrance fills the air?
Have you known a heartfelt yearning?
Known release from trying care?

Have you wandered through the wildwood
By a laughing little stream?
As you watched the waters dancing
Did you dream a little dream?

Many joys you've found out walking,
Should the answer not be nay,
By the wildwood, gird with beauty,
In the early month of May.

Charles Ruggles Fox

My Garden

My garden gives me so much joy.
When dear friends come to call,
I like to have them view my flow'rs
Along my garden wall.

I've buttercups as bright as gold
And peonies of red,
While in the springtime tulips wear
Bright turbans on their head.

There are hollyhocks against a fence
And black-eyed Susans, too,
While pink geraniums raise their heads
To get a better view.

And in a corner daisies bloom
As brightly as the sun,
While violets in a shady nook
Look bashful, every one.

I share my garden with my friends
That they might share with me
The joy I feel in growing flow'rs
That last in memory.

Carice Williams

Walking in a Garden

A garden gate that freely swings,
A robin redbreast taking wing,
There's lasting comfort and repose—
While walking in a garden.

Flowers blossom everywhere,
Their fragrance fills the air.
Woes and worries are effaced
As nature's beauty I embrace—
While walking in a garden.

Brow and cheek are softly teased
By a warm and gentle breeze,
God's wonders never cease
To instill a sense of peace—
While walking in a garden.

Florence B. Kennedy

Ideals Remembers the Way It Used to Be

Do you remember sitting on the porch, just watching the world pass by? Or when washing clothes was an all-day affair with boiling kettles and a hand-turned wringer? Do you remember the fashions started by Charles Gibson and his Gibson girls?

Ideals does, and in our next issue, Old-Fashioned Ideals, we recall some of the best days of our past. Join us as we take a look at some manners which have changed permanently, children's games which have stayed the same, and a few customs which may just need to be revived. Why not share these memories with a gift subscription, starting with Old-Fashioned Ideals.

ACKNOWLEDGEMENTS

MOTHER AND HER SECRET by Al Capp, used with permission of the Estate of Alfred G. Capp; GRANDMOTHER'S QUILT from *A MONTH OF MONDAYS* by Mary Lou Carney, copyright © 1984 by Abingdon Press, used by permission; WHEN GOD CREATED SUN AND STARS by Katherine Edelman, reprinted by permission of Katherine Edelman Lyon, literary executrix for Katherine Edelman; LIKE MOTHER USED TO MAKE by Marjorie Holmes, reprinted by permission of The McCall Publishing Company; NEW MOTHER'S SONG from *PETALS OF LIGHT* by Jane Merchant, copyright © 1958 assigned to Abingdon Press, used by permission; TOMORROW I'LL CLEAN THE ATTIC from *I NEEDED THE QUIET AND OTHER POEMS* by Alice Hansche Mortenson, Kansas City, MO: Beacon Hill Press of Kansas City, copyright © 1978; A MOTHER'S MEMORY from *AN OLD CRACKED CUP* by Margaret Rorke, copyright © 1980 by Northwood Institute Press. Our sincere thanks to the following authors whose addresses we were unable to locate: B.S. Gillilan for THE READING MOTHER by Strickland Gillilan; Roy Z. Kemp for DAFFODILS; Florence B. Kennedy for WALKING IN A GARDEN; Verna Sparks for INSIDE MY GARDEN GATE; Clyde Edwin Tuck for THE SONGS MY MOTHER SANG from *VOICES IN THE WIND*, copyright 1950 by Clyde Edwin Tuck; W. Earlington Whitney for A LOAF OF MOTHER'S BREAD from *REVERIES OF THE OLD HOMESTEADER*, copyright © 1946 by W. Earlington Whitney.